SOUL ON THE LINE

Michael John Pike (Spike)

Printed in Great Britain by
Bramble Press 2012

ISBN 978-0-9556984-4-6

6

Michael John Pike (Spike) was born in Glasgow (or just ootside) – Served five years in the Army (First Battalion Scots Guards) – Now lives in Corby where he has established himself as a writer and performance poet. Many of his poems are a reflection of himself and his view on humanity.

INTRODUCTION

I started writing poetry a few years after leaving the Scots Guards. Like most Ex Service Personnel, it took many years to adjust to civilian life.

Drink and drugs seemed to be the order of the day. This way of life went on for nearly 20 years, glad to say I no longer live that way. I'm more at peace with myself than at any time in my life.

Why did it take so long - I don't know! I read a book by Dr Wayne Dyer – Change Your Thoughts, Change Your Life.

It's Dr Dyer's interpretation of the Tao Te Ching. While reading it, I came across this gem by Witter Bynner 1944; this is his translation of the 53rd verse of the Tao.

It blew me away...Enjoy, Spike.

See how fine the palaces
And see how poor the farms
How bare the peasants granaries
While gentry wear embroideries
Hiding sharpened arms
The more they have, the more they seize
How can there be such men as these
Who never hunger, never thirst
Yet eat and drink until they burst

Anyone looking for spiritual guidance, I strongly recommend Dr Wayne Dyer's Book - Change Your Thoughts, Change Your Life.

Michael John Pike
(Spike)
2012

WAR, POLITICS AND RELIGION

LAYER CAKE

Parade our heroes
With drums and flutes
Behind it all
Are men in suits

Give nothing back
For all they take
It's all about
The layer of cake

Displaying banners
Flying high
For fighting souls
The end is nigh

For the cake is fat
And fatter grows
Ever increasing
The death toll rolls

Giving orders
From behind a desk
And drink a toast
Oh! How they're blessed

They don't care
For all the dying
To keep them rich
They continue lying

They need the troops
So young and healthy
To give their blood
And keep them wealthy

It's time to stop
For heaven's sake
And end for once
The layer cake

OH DEAR HOW SAD NEVER MIND

Why the hue and cry
The rich could end up broke
They want us all to bail them out
On crocodile tears they choke

Please dig deep you peasants
No cash, we have no clout
Help us to refill the trough
Where for years we've had our snout

Fine clothes, expensive jewellery
Hide a multitude of sin
But the debts are mounting up
Like empties in an alkies bin

So go and take a run and jump
We've no interest in your plight
We work for everything we've got
So tough it serves you right

So time to let the silver go
And pawn expensive cars
No cash to large it up
Or drink in trendy bars

The way you squandered all that cash
Was sheer complacency
Now the lesson life is sending you
Is called humility

BLOODIED KISS

Kings and Presidents
They start the wars
But never bear the soldiers' scars
The troops assembled from the masses
Recruited from the lower classes
To spill their blood
In some foreign ditch
To keep those filthy bastards rich
Since time began
It's been like this
On the cheeks of children
A bloodied kiss
Another family father missed

But we beat the drum
And bands will play
March them off to war
     HOORAY
The days, the months
The war just drags
The dead come home
In body bags
They spilt their blood
In some foreign ditch
To keep those filthy bastards rich

Those who return
For peace they yearn
But those filthy bastards
Never learn

CHAOS, JUST ROUND THE BEND

We have it oh, so easy
Everything at hand
Produce ever growing
Shelves are overflowing
For any kind of brand
A network of busy-busy
People scurry to and fro
Massive supermarkets
Where families come and go
What if the network halted
The busy-busy stopped
Empty supermarkets
Where thousands once had shopped
Unrest would lead to riots
As families fight for food
Prepared to kill and injure
Just to feed their brood
As the masses march and throng
With anger, raised fist clenched
Driven by a need to feed
Thirst and hunger drenched
When a soldier, fed
Aims his gun to shoot
At those through panic
Driven to loot
The sound of gunfire
Fills the street
We fall to our knees
In blood-soaked defeat
Only then will we
Realise
We are not so advanced, or
Civilised

FALLEN HEROES

The sun comes up to cast its warmth
On a remembrance parade
To all our fallen heroes
A meaningless charade

Hoof on cobble, beast well brushed
The bones of fallen heroes crushed
Shiny leather, bayonets gleam
Mass bands start up to hide
A fallen hero's scream

And royals in red tunic dressed
With Poundland medals on their chest
The dignitaries with sombre face
Clad in suit and tie
As fly-by fighter jets
Corrupt the peaceful sky

With heads low bowed
March past the crowd
The living soldiers breathe
Lay at the Cenotaph
A poppy guilt red wreath

Salute the mothers
Who felt the pain
The ones who suffered most
Weep for our fallen heroes
Now a band of ghosts
Lest we forget
Let's drink a toast
Our fallen heroes
Our band of ghosts

A MOTHER'S TEARS

Fifteen young men
Fly home dead in a plane
Casualties all
Of a world gone insane

She knew what was coming
When she answered the door
The news hit her hard
And she fell to the floor

Painfully sobbing
A Mum's broken heart
Another family
So ripped apart

She thinks of the field
Where her Son bled
Then thinks of the baby
She once breast fed

She remembers the boy
That she nurtured in growth
He grew then took
That military oath

A young man, strong
Able and willing
Seduced by the call
And took the Queen's shilling

A Mother kneels broken
As She smells her Son's clothes
Then on his coffin
She placed a red rose

This is the week that Britain lost 15 service personnel; none of the deceased
were children of the politicians who sent these young people to War.

HISTORY

History is written
by brutal evil men
once they'd bloodied up their sword
they sought to use the pen

To tell their version of events
about brave battles fought
but all their lands and titles
were flesh and murder bought

Who will write the history
of the African slave
or write the book that tells the plight
of the Indian Brave

Who will talk about the Celts
burned by Christian hands
or the many that were stoned to death
by barbaric Islamic demands

Now to write things presently
well nothing's changed at all
what's going on now, has happened then
empires rise and fall

The care and sophistication
spent on weapons that we build
the hundred years of discard
in the land sites that were filled

How do we tell our children
about the poisoned seas
or what happened to the wildlife
the plants, the shrubs, the trees

How the hell will we explain
why we can't breathe without a mask
who will write that history
for someone quite a task

But I really need not worry
by then we'll all be gone
our planet will be like Venus
baked by a scornful sun

Well done!

HURRY, SCURRY, DEAD

Always in a hurry
Getting nowhere fast
Don't hurry getting anywhere
Be happy coming last
Why do we beat the sidewalks
At such a frantic pace
A desperate need to lead
The daily human race
Buy food, no time to wait
I need it now, to go
And in a paper cup
Take away, espresso
Must catch the bus
To get the train
Or get there faster
Go by plane
We are indeed a race insane
We need to learn to slow it down
Not be in such a hurry
And cut down on the stress
Anxiety and worry
Do corpses in the cemetery
Hurry to and fro'
No…it's all serenity and peace
There's nothing there 'to go'

JULIAN ASSANGE

They're going to get you
Hunt you down
They're going to drive you
Underground
They're coming from all angles
And going to smear your name
Create a raging fire
From a non-existent flame
How dare you try expose them
For the evil that they are
You have no place to hide
Their network stretches far
They can make the biggest lie
Suddenly appear
Or make the greatest truth, like you
Quietly disappear

OLD FIRM

Marching blindly
To tunes of hate
March to different banners
Thus we separate

Become fragmented
From each other
Street against street
House against house
Brother against brother

History was written
By men with no vision
No eyes and no heart
It's those lies that tear societies
Families and lives apart

They penned their poison
The dye was cast
Living lives through hatred
Killing for the past

Put down those banners
Your flutes and guns
There is no division
No Feniens, no Huns

To the bigots and morons
A message to all
Let's stop all the fighting
And just kick a ball

RELIGIOUS LIMERICK

Oh! The masses they reach
For the people that preach
To me it's all just a racket
They're up to their knees
In dodgy wee deals
And making an absolute packet

There're Popes smoking dope
Suits snorting coke
Nuns with a habit
With their rampant rabbit

Evangelist, Baptist
Methodist and captives
More teams than the premier league
It's all based on a lie
About spirits that fly
And all the bad shit
To come when we're dead

Will I fry for God's sake
In a deep burning lake
If I happen to play with my willie
Or think about sex
Oh! how perplex
The whole thing is just a bit silly

Only the good will prevail
To heaven they sail
The rest of us all face the devil
You can all go and fuck
I'm trusting in luck
So sit on my finger and swivel

JUST A MAN

Hero to zero
In the blink of a salute
Here have some medals
And a blood soaked de-mob suit
We thank you for courage
Whilst in the rank and file
But you're damaged and no use to us
Now you face your toughest mile
So kindly go, don't look back
And don't start asking why
We've thousands more young men to train
Many more to die
We need them for the wars we wage
Invading foreign soil
It all comes down to money
It all comes down to oil
You've done your bit
For Queen and God
Now go and find yourself a job
But you'll rant and rave
To all around
That once you were a force
Still no-one will employ you
And your wife files for divorce
Now you wrestle with the guilt
You were only doing your duty
Riddled with the memories
And bullets of self pity
So now you're all alone
To clutch an empty glass
Trying to reconstruct your life
Praying for this pain to pass

Once you were a soldier
Marching strong and proud
In your closet hangs a uniform
Now a meaningless shroud
They geared you up for war
To fight the Arab, Paddy, Hun
After years of bloodshed
Your soul is on the run
All the bullshit that you swallowed
Now begins to choke
You smoke another cigarette
Drink J D and coke
The fighting's got to stop
That's raging in your head
But there's no-one there
To comfort you
Your relationships, all dead
So what do you do
End it now
Or learn to heal your pain
And leave the lies behind you
To be a man again

THE PRICE

Come young people
Heed the call
In distant lands
To fight and fall
You have the courage
We have the guns
To sacrifice
The masses' sons
By turning red
The mud and soil
For blood is now
The price of oil

Support our heroes
Wear a band
And fry their souls
On burning sand
Sent to war
By suited fools
To lie in blood
Guilt ridden pools
By turning red
The mud and soil
For blood is now
The price of oil

The politicians lie and lie
More and more
The soldiers die
While devastated
families cry
We're left to ask the
question
WHY?
To ask that question
There is no need
It all comes down
To human greed
By turning red
The mud and soil
For blood is now
The price of oil

The soldiers sweat
They graft they toil
Their blood is now
The price of oil

ALLOW LIFE TO FLOW

Why do we feel the need
To be somewhere that we're not
Or feel the need to have
Something we've not got

Why do we bemoan the thought
That life is so unfair
And blindly stumble through each day
Grasping at thin air

Yet life can be so easy
If we live it day by day
And feel that we're just actors
In life's elaborate play

And a script that has been written
We win, we love, we lose
But we can rewrite the script
Any time we choose

We're only here to learn
How to live, to love, to grow
We can't grasp onto life
Just leave it, let it flow

The Wind Blows Then Goes

Behind the darkest
Most threatening cloud
There's sunshine
And clear sky

The aftermath of a storm
That blew roofs away
And ripped up trees
Brings serenity and calm

If nature can't sustain such anger
How much less can man

SAND

Even the highest mountain
even the toughest rock
even hard grey granite
or even soft white chalk

Yet no matter how tall
no matter how grand
it all breaks down
it all becomes sand

You could be a king
you could be a queen
you could be the greatest
there's ever been

But life like the sands
slips through our hands

All our ambitions
all that we planned
all becomes dust
all becomes sand

WHEN WE'RE GONE

Nothing on earth will grieve
When we eventually leave
Nothing on earth will mourn
When we are finally gone

Will the fish in the river
Or the birds in the sky
Look at each other
And think to ask why?

Will the tree ask the badger
Where did they go?
They won't ask the question
For they don't even know

They would look at each other
And probably say
The planet feels
So much safer today

I'M AT PEACE

I'm at peace when I look
At life clearly
There's no clutter
No fighting
No guns

I'm at peace when my heart
Beats so gently
There's no TV
No shouting
No bombs

I'm at peace when our souls
Dance with nature
There's no pollution
No hunger
No slums

I'm at peace when I see
No division
No religion
No countries
We're one

CRADLE TO GRAVE (IN BRIEF)

When I was forced
From the warm security
Of my mother's womb

To spend a lifetime
My imprisoned soul
In a physical tomb

A term of self-obsession
To find out
What is real

A lifetime finding out
What it is to feel

That honesty of self
Beyond the flesh and bone

Beyond disease, decay and death
As we make our way
Back home

GOLD

When the earth dries up
Turn up the heat
Our Self destruction
Now complete

The fields are bare
Not even weeds
Nothing that breathes
Nothing that bleeds

A septic ocean
Ebb's to and fro'
Just emptiness
With nothing to show

No birds, no fish
No cows, no sheep
Just all the gold
That we can eat

REALITY CHECK

The more real life gets for me
The more insane things seem to be

I just don't get the human race
They cannot see beyond their face

Instant access, H/D, fast food
Overlooking all that's good

At my fingertips all to know
Wrap up my life, I'll have it to go

Nature's bounty all laid before
But still not happy we all want more

We think we're smart, we think we're clever
We think our race will go on forever

I observe mankind and shake my head
Is this the reason so many bled

To make us fat to make us greedy
To make us selfish and oh, so needy

Yes the more real life gets for me
The more insane things seem to be

TEARS

I can't deny, I often cry
those tears that fall
and cleanse my face
They dull the glare
untie the knots
those tears that roll
in tiny drops
They only last a little while
then it's time for me to smile

NATURE

The rain it falls to slake the land
Going to and from the sky
The buzz of life is all around
Nature does and does not try

It's only humans in a race
Nature knows the gentle pace
But in a second
All changes course
By wind and water
Such a force
Slaying all
With no remorse

Then just as quick
All's calm and still
For nature can, and nature will

Have no fear of nature's cycle
Or shake your fist and cry
It's nature's way of doing things
We're born, we live, we die

So when our heart stops beating
The soul will still remain
And return to an earthly body
Time and time again

THE BOX

Everything I vowed I'd never be
I have become
Everything I ever was
I now despise
This journey of a thousand mistakes
Then I realise

There's no fanfare
No first prize
No motherly figure
To dry our eyes

Just a body showing scars
Of a thousand knocks
Bent over shuffling
Arthritic old crocks
Remains wept over
Carted off in a box

Where will I leave my mark
Shall I spray on a wall
Pee on a tree
Create a beautiful work of art
For everyone to see

I think every human's basic fear
Who will know I was ever here

Are we just bent over
Arthritic old crocks
Remains wept over
Carted off in a box

THE OWL

Veils of sun
Pierce the grey cloud
Setting time for night to fall
Dark...for the owl to call

The veils have gone
Where the sun had shone
Stars pierce the night time sky
Dark...for the owl to fly

Rodents now crawl
Down a woodland trail
They sniff, they forage, they scratch
Dark...for the owl to catch

Terror screams loud
Through the night mist air
Swift of claw with belly to fill
Dark...for the owl to kill

Night gives way to dawn
As sun starts to shine
A night of hunting blessed
Light...for the owl to rest

FATHER TIME

There're seven signs from Father Time
That says we're getting old
And getting old is such a crime
How often are we told

So much time and energy
As we fret against the clock
Instead of just enjoying
What little time we've got

For the ageing process started
The moment we were born
The days, the weeks, the years
Become a twisting thorn

Our lives are like the morning mist
That vanishes at noon
The years they go so very fast
It's over all to soon

All the surgery and the ointments
That somehow half the years
Are designed to keep us spending
And thus compound our fears

So forgive that little wrinkle
Have in your eye a twinkle
And embrace those living years

THE PATH

Making this journey
Through the eyes of a fool
Not knowing which corner to turn
This path that I'm on
Seems so narrowed and thorned
And the souls of my feet often burn

This weight that I carry
Are thoughts from the past
The burden of guilt and of sorrow
Walk with me a while
Share this load for a mile
I'll maybe feel lighter tomorrow

The path feels more even
Not so narrowed and thorned
We'll rest up just round the next bend
The load's so much lighter
The day so much brighter
For soon this journey will end

The end, for soon all our journeys will end

TO ALL A TOAST

There's no such thing as self-made
Or self-made millionaire
We're all dependent on each other
We depend on human care

We depend so much on everyone
All the folk we never see
A whole network of love
For without we could not be

So raise our glass

To the folk that drive the lorries
Mend the roads and work the mill
The folk that stack the shelves
Sweep the streets and ring the till

The folk that drive the taxis
The buses and the trains
The folk that issue tickets
Stamp the passports, fly the planes

The folk that work at A&E
That patch us when we bleed
The folk that care and comfort
All the folk in need

The folk I say hello to
When I'm up the town
The folk that smile and pick me up
When I'm feeling down

To the folk I haven't mentioned
Thank you, you heed the call
To each and every human being
A toast to one and all

TV...PUB...WORK

Tiny little red brick cave
Inside, a TV-shackled slave
I think I'll make a cup of tea
Kitchen bound, two minutes free
For real release there is the pub
Or round the bend the social club
Depression there it goes much deeper
But what the hell the drinks are cheaper
Pint in hand, cloud over head
Wondering why you feel so dead
Then off to work to earn a wage
And write another sorry page
Of nothing, nothing, nothing to say
Nothing of interest happened today
Or any day, fall to my knees and pray
There's got to be more inside I scream
Than watching movement on a plasma screen
I return each night
To my red brick cave
And remain a TV-shackled slave

TV...PUB...WORK

Tiny little red brick cave
Inside a TV shackled slave
I think I'll make a cup of tea
Kitchen bound, two minutes free
For real release there... is the pub
Or round the bend the soaps... club
Depression there it goes much deeper
Put in hand, cloud over head
Then off to work to earn a wage
And write another sorry page
Of nothing, nothing, nothing to say
Nothing of interest happened today
Or any day, fall to my knees and pray
There's got to be more inside I scream

BRIAN

Hi Brian
It's everyone that knows you

We hear you've discarded
your physical being

There's nothing now
to stop from seeing

The beauty surrounding
the spirit you're freeing

We'll miss your laugh
We'll miss your smile
We're glad you stayed
With us a while

To all of us
this day will come
Together we'll dance
and be as one

(To Brian Walker)

CLOSE THE DOOR

Please stop clogging up my attic
I don't want you there no more
So put on your shoes, step outside
And quietly close the door

You overstay your welcome
With nothing new to say
You've cleaned me out of food and drink
Now kindly go away

Keep walking, don't look back
There's nothing you've forgot
I have no time to entertain
Such a nasty little thought

It's a daily grind I find
To keep the attic free of sin
For the minute I drop my guard
Bad thoughts come flooding in

So stop clogging up my headspace
You're not welcome anymore
Put on your shoes, get your coat
And quietly close the door

IMAGES

Images of violence
Flick
In my mind's eye
Faces contort
That look of hate
I close myself to the reason why

I've tasted the anger
Kicked out in spite
I understand
Why young men fight

I've felt those feelings
Drawn those looks
I release it now
By reading books

So I wander back
Every now and then
Feel the fire that burns
Within most men

Is it tribal, religion or man kind's hate
Will it all come down to simple fate
Has our time expired
For running the show
With my hand on my heart
I really don't know

KILL OR CURE

There is no truth
It does not lie
It does not accuse
It doesn't ask why
You can't make deals
No plea and no bargain
Ask it for leniency
Or beg its pardon
It is what it is
In its own way
When we succumb
To disease and decay
That's why I choose
To embrace what is now
To seize the moment
Live it and how
To breathe every second
Feel every beat
Have the sun on my back
And the snow at my feet
Exhale the air
On a cold frosty day
Splash through a puddle
And let myself play
Dance, wave my arms
Look around me and smile
In this body I'll stay
At least for a while

MUM

She was the warmth to wake us
Gently shake us from our dreams

Make sure we all had breakfast
Amid the squabbles and the screams

She always taught us manners
Say thank you and say please

Always there to pick us up
When we fell and skint our knees

The one to reassure
When one of us would cry

She was the silk soft tissue
To dry a tear-stained eye

She was the stars, the moon
The wind, the sun

The finest woman
She was our Mum

(Written on behalf of a friend)

MY BODY

Try to nourish and water
what my body needs

Try to stem the flow
when my body bleeds

Try to understand
when I'm weak and cry

Knowing that it's just the flesh
for the spirit shall always fly

STILL THE MOUTH

I have nothing to say
Today
Nothing delightful
Or insightful
No words of the wise
Or phrase to despise
No world changing comment
Or gentle lament
I'll put down my pen
Take a walk through the fen
Just enjoy this fine day
For I've nothing to say

THE ENEMY WITHIN

Your horns don't have the power
To penetrate my chest
Your talons are not sharp enough
To tear and rip my flesh
Those threats and angry insults
Fall weakly at my feet
With so much negativity
You'll never be complete

I've looked into your eyes
I see a man in so much pain
That's why
I have unclenched my fist
And act with such restrain

Throughout all your hostility
It's clear for me to see
That I represent the man
The man you long to be

PATCHWORK POEM

Welcome to our patchwork theory
And how we view our world
From when we lived inside the womb
All warm and cozy-curled

Then we were born, as infants grew
And looked with innocent eyes
Then realised that what we saw
Was built on greed and lies

That's how we formed our patchwork theory
Our patchwork look at life

There's so much we are not sure of
As the years go rolling by
We have wisdom and yes! Humour
But our tanks are almost dry

We've learned of grace and manners
To let go, not push and shove
That money's not important
All we really need is love

That's how we formed our patchwork theory
Our patchwork look at life

Our journey's thorned and littered
On a cracked uneven path
So many times we've fallen
Where we've bled, we cried, we laughed

It's not that we are boring
We've just learned to take it easy
Just enjoy what nature offers
To walk the bright and breezy

That's how we formed our patchwork theory
Our patchwork look at life

We no longer get excited
About who done this and that
X factor, soaps and media
It's all a load of tatt

Will Andy win the tennis
Or what's the final score
There's nothing that's outside of us
In our hearts there's so much more

That's how we formed our patchwork theory
Our patchwork look at life

The ravages of time
Are being etched upon our brow
We smile about the past
And live the here and now

Not brag about our winnings
Or moan about our loss
Things are all so clear now
We really couldn't give a toss

That's how we formed our patchwork theory
Our patchwork look at life

THE WAKE

Mourners gather in threadbare suits
Don a tie and shiny boots
Solemn handshakes
Deadpan looks

Pay homage to a friend
Through drink he passed away
A quickie at the crem'
Then get pissed all day

To all the assembled here
I'd like to buy a round
Please help me with the drinks
Oh! and tap me twenty pound

Going through the motions
Talking rights and wrongs
Cry and hug each other
While singing drunken songs

With bleary eyes, and loosened ties
All filled with pain and sorrow
Best we put this wake to bed
There's another one tomorrow

MAY YOURS

May yours be the last lips
I ever choose to kiss
May yours be the last heartbeat
I ever choose to miss
May yours be the last skin
I lovingly caress
May you be the last woman
I ever watch undress
May yours be the last eyes
I gaze into at night
And may ours be the last embrace
Wrapped up in the warm sunlight

TRAIL OF BREAD

Even through your agony
Your anger and despair
I want you now, to know my friend
I love you and I care
You're wandering in the wilderness
Chasing shadows in your head
The demon birds have eaten
Your well laid trail of bread
I know the emptiness you're feeling
Abandoned and alone
So take my hand, I'm here
Let's make our way back home

WILLIE

Willie Berry, the magic man,
convince your mind,
with feint of hand.
Things disappear, then, reappear
this way, that way,
behind your ear.
It's magic, clever, not a lie,
create illusion
to deceive the eye.
To a magic moment,
he'll take you there,
producing items
from thin air.
Step up, kind sir,
please take the stand,
Corby's wondrous magic man.

YOU

If I could hear soft whispers in my ear
Like a gentle hand across my brow
To wipe away my fear

If I could feel the sun upon my face
The smell of honeysuckle
That lovely summer grace

If I could feel the rain run through my hair
Or jump from branch to branch
And play a game of dare

If I could paddle barefoot in a river
And feel your presence in my life
Forever

If I could wake each day and drink the morning dew
If I could make all that a person
It surely would be you

CORBY TOWN

There's a Town somewhere in England
Built from the grinders wheel
Grew from digging ore and the folk that made the steel
And the light from the Corby candle shone
That lit the sky from dusk till dawn

And the town grew bigger still, by the hands of the hardy folk
That grafted out a living, amongst the noise and smoke
But then the works were closed, many a tear was shed
For it's hard to set a table with little meat and bread

But we carry on regardless, with music song and dance
Ok the works are gone; it was never our last stance
Now many a different culture arriving in our town
Most will welcome with open arms and ignore the bigot's frown

So most of us came through, played with the hand been dealt
For Corby has a pulse, just crying out to be felt

DANIEL

Take it from my silence
There's nothing more to say
The leaving of a loved one
Pain's the price to pay
He's my friend, my bud, my laugh mate
My one my only son
We've barely been apart since his life begun

He's grown now and knows his mind
It's time to fly the nest
I know it's going to break my heart
But I know I've done my best
The joy of being a parent
My cup forever full
Then it's time to say goodbye
Life at times is cruel
Would I change the script of life
To save me from this pain
Not a chance, I'll take the blow
For I'd do it all again

MY SISTER DEE

He chose to walk
At a more gentle pace
And started to wear
Fine silk and lace

Tired of hiding
And living a sham
Tired of life
And being a man

Dressed like a lady
Walks late at night
Full of desire
And filled with fright

It was time to stand up
Let the woman come through
And face all the bigots
Just to be true

So that's what she did
He became she
I'm so very proud
Of my big Sister Dee

A.M. - PRISON BITCH

The coward King he is
He's doing life now, bless
Pulled his usual stunt
This time kicked a man to death

He put one guy in a wheelchair
Kicked him till he bled
Then showing no humanity
Left him there for dead

Now he's locked up in his cell
A room so small and sparse
Allegedly bends over now
And takes it up the arse

Bet he was shaking
While standing in the dock
He's now the prison bitch
And wears a pretty frock

A.M. - PRISON BITCH

The coward king he is
He's going life now, hiss
Pulled his usual stunt
This time kicked a man to death.

He put one guy in a wheelchair
Kicked him till he bled
Then showing no humanity,
Left him there for dead

Now he's locked up in his cell
A room so small and sparse
Allegedly bends over now
And takes it up the arse

But he was shaking
While standing in the dock
He's now the prison bitch,
And wears a pretty frock

COLLEGE TERROR

A power crazy woman
a bad tempered bitch
The college evil resident
a really nasty witch
She loves to cast her spells
turning wee boys into frogs
then stirring septic potions
turns pretty girls to dogs
Lurking in the shadows
like an angry troll
and a face that would grace
any totem pole
All the staff at College
tremble in her wake
we should try her, tie her up
and burn her at the stake
Then sweep up all the ashes
while the devil tolls her bell
then send the bitch packing
all the way to HELL

(Most of us have worked for or had a boss that was a tyrant.
This is about one such person)

GOSSIP, RUMOUR, SCANDAL

Rumour has it, I was told
Oh! I heard this and that
Don't the gossips leave you cold?
It's all just tittle-tatt

I was told by someone
That someone else said this
So I said something else to them
Who said they took the piss

So rumour has it she was told
Who said the same to me
This was said by such and such
Therefore it has to be

So when I spoke to thingy
Who told me of her wrath
That how her neighbour lets her dog
Go poo-poo on the path

Is that really all they've got
To get them through the day
I don't believe a single word
Those morons have to say

This rumour mill just doesn't stop
Another scandal, name to drop

Chit, chit, chit
Chat, chat, chat
Yadda, yadda, yadda,
Crap, crap, crap

So I heard this and you heard that
It's what we heard today
This is how they go through life
Until they're old and grey

Wey hey

ODE TO A BEAN

The humble bean
Oh, how we poke
And laugh about
A windy joke

Often women
Swear to this
That they would never
Release a whiff

It's the girly way
The farts delivered
They let them go
In carpet slippers

Tho' it's true
Oh humble bean
All packed with goodness
And protein

While in a crowd
The laugh will start
When one lets rip
A mighty fart

The laughter grows
The smell is scattered
And leave the sphincter
Worn and tattered

So loud or silent
It's all the same
We all indulge
In the farting game

The resulting smell
Is foul and rank
To the humble bean
We truly thank

SEXY CHEF

Loads of shows
On how to cook
By sexy chefs
That don't use a book

Nigella Lawson
Hits the heights
With little nibbles
And lustful bites

Lorraine Pascal
Makes steamed sea bass
With smouldering eyes
And a gorgeous ass

Watch how we stroke
The pepper pot
Now careful guys
The ovens HOT!!!

Now add the flavour
In little bits
A serving suggestion
Just shake your tits

Food's hard to prepare
Or even plan
When you're cracking one off
To honey roast ham

With sensual strokes
And pouting lips
Stuffing the birds
With hands on hips

There's men in aprons
Seducing haddock
Much has changed
Since Fanny Craddock

So let's raise our glass
To the girls with the most
For now it's sexy
To make beans on toast

THE RAVENS

Ravens of the airways
or Corby radio
Whether it is day or night
they're putting on a show

Ravens of the airways
bring music, news, and chat
By tuning into Corby folk
about, Oh! This and that

Ravens of the airways
if it's local then it matters
It could be something serious
or a joke about mad hatters

Ravens of the airways
always playing your part
A spirit of community
Corby's beating heart

DRINK AND DRUGS

BEATEN LASS

There's a poor wee soul
outside the store
Hood up, crouched over and beaten
she looks up, god bless
her face is a mess
Hood up, crouched over and beaten
To get what she needs
her body she sells
the same undernourished
body that smells
Hood up, crouched over and beaten
It's the smell of the street
It's the smell of defeat
Hood up, crouched over and beaten
What kind of life is she living
What kind of food does she eat
she's off as she planned
bottle in hand
back to her nightmare retreat
Hood up crouched over and beaten

THE PARTY'S OVER

Suicide comes up with the sun
When the drink and drugs are done
Flat is stinking, mirror smashed
Look around the place is trashed
Beer cans strewn on a dog-end floor
Looking like an oil slick shore
Poppin' pills, snorting coke
God I think I'm gonna choke
Downing so much alcohol
Oh! the carpet broke my fall
Look at myself with quiet rebuke
Scrape off my face dried up puke
Yes
Suicide comes up with the sun
When the drink and drugs are done

DRUNKS

Grey eyed
Grey haired
Grey clad sad men
Cluster smoking
Coughing choking

The pub is where they're at
They go there every day
To drink to smoke to chat

Then they head home penniless
And breathe a drunken sigh
They make that journey every day
Until the day they die

SKAG DRESSED UP

You cheat, you liar, you parasite
You uncompromising tart
Snorting your way through society
Tearing lives apart

You rob, you steal, you're a drunk at the wheel
You never buy your round
And when my wallet's empty
You're nowhere to be found

You sexed me up said you were a friend
Then you drove me round the bend
You're a fake on the take
You plunder and you loot

All you are cocaine
Is heroin in a suit

FANCY A BEER

Sitting at a bar
Not looking out of place
Wheezing thro' your smoke filled lungs
And alcohol ravaged face
There's merriment and laughter
But the thirst cannot be quenched
The mood can change so very quick
As a drunken fist is clenched
Then tempers flare
With an aggressive stare
Which then turns into violent glare
Jostling, pushing, voices raised
A drink is thrown by a spouse enraged

It all comes down to heavy drinking
Dysfunctional lives
And negative thinking

Yes, this is man at his drunken worst
Then the guilt, the drinker's curse

REMEMBER

Remember how bad it felt
When last you had a drink
The sweats the cramps the shits
How badly did that stink

Remember how bad it felt
When last you had cocaine
Shaking, rattling, raging
I bought myself a bag of pain

Remember why you feel so good
With exercise and decent food
Now remember how it felt before
When you were knocking on madness door

So when you leave your safety place
Greet all you meet
With warmth and grace
Meet eye with eye
And smile with smile
Knowing you'll go that extra mile

So hey well done
What more can I say
Without booze without coke
You got thro' the day

NO MORE

No more for me the pub
Where I held my council dear
No more for me the spending
And scoring dodgy gear
No more the drunken laughter
That hid my silent pain
No more my life and sanity
Slipping down the drain

No more the football banter
and playing games of pool
No more snorting coke
and acting like a fool
No more waking up
and wishing I was dead
No more storms of lunacy
raging in my head

No more lonely nights
praying for pain to end
No more drink and drugs
to drive me round the bend
I've seen and done my final round
The end
The end
The end

STARVE THE BEAST

What a lovely feeling
Free from drugs and drink
Everything so bright
And how clearly now I think
It's like my soul's been cleansed
From an all consuming cancer
Now I'm in control
Like a well trained ballet dancer
I feel I've paid my dues
To fat cat money makers
That thrive on people's misery
Lowlife, scumbag heartbreakers

Now cigarettes, I ask
How the hell can they be legal
The graveyard is full of corpses
Gunned down by Embassy Regal

And alcohol for heaven's sake
The profits run to billions
And devastate so many lives
That run to countless millions

But they need to keep us spending
To make their profits soar
That's why it's called addiction
It leaves us needing more

So we need a revolution
To make their profits drop
Let's put our heads together
And collectively...

JUST STOP

HOPE

In life we will experience,
disappointment loss and death.
There are times we feel
we can't go on, when tired
and out of breath.
There are times of quiet despair,
of suffering and of pain,
when we seem to stack up losses
and very little gain.
There are times we feel defeated,
ridiculed and small,
but a ray of hope
in one wee triumph,
can overcome it all.

HOPE

In life we will experience
disappointment loss and death
There are times we feel
we can't go on, when tired
and out of breath
There are times of quiet despair
of suffering and of pain,
when we seem to stack up losses
and very little gain.
There are times we feel defeated
but a ray of hope